Reading & Writing For Every Child

D1742069

Teacher Manual

by

Paula Van Kuren

Every child deserves the opportunities that reading and writing afford. Each child is full of hope, talent, and a drive to live and learn. In a world mapped out with words, it is only through mastery of those words that the child can grow and thrive. Without the understanding of how our language works, without the ability to communicate in both oral and written language, a child is cut off from the wealth of our culture. This book is my attempt at granting to children a simple method for learning the most vital of all academic skills, reading and writing. May all who use this book use their skills and talent to do good in our world.

Learning "quirks" have been a central part of my personal homeschooling journey since I began teaching my oldest in 2007. Because we did not have the resources to outsource his learning, and the public school options we had at the time were abysmal, I poured out my energy into learning how to teach my child to read and write in spite of the struggle. There are many philosophies and methodologies that claim to be the one sure way to get a child (even a dyslexic child) reading and writing. I spent hours, days, weeks, months, years, working out these programs. When they didn't work for my son, I studied deeper. I tried harder. We worked more. The more we worked, however, the more we extinguished the desire to learn in my son. He was trying hard, working hard, and his best efforts were not giving him the happy result of reading his favorite books. If I was working hard and he was working hard, then the problem had to be somewhere else. Thus began my expedition for a method of teaching literacy that would work for my son and for other children who struggle. The pedagogy of literacy is a passion that I'm pouring into creating resources that ease the path to success.

My method for teaching reading and writing may look complex, with many parts and pieces to keep going throughout the lessons, but the core idea is simple. The idea that we are building up the sub-skills needed for fluent reading and writing guides every activity. When all of the sub-skills are in place and in working order, reading and writing are FUN! When even one sub-skill is lacking, reading and writing become a chore and a frustration. Reading and writing are two very different, but interconnected skills. Sometimes dyslexic students are able to overcome the reading hurdle through self-coping techniques (which require high intelligence, I might add), but their dyslexia shines through when it comes to spelling and writing. Their verbal communication development might be years ahead of their chronological age, while their written communication lags woefully behind. This first book builds those basic skills slowly and methodically in order to prevent those painful gaps later on.

Reading aloud to your child is arguably the most important thing you can do for their literacy development. I will write another book another day about how reading aloud to your child feeds their hearts, minds, and souls. In this Teacher Manual, I will focus on the literacy skills built by hearing the written words spoken aloud. Reading aloud is the most effective (and most pleasant!) method of vocabulary development for a child. Hearing it pronounced, hearing it used in context, and hearing the nuances in the reader's voice all give the listener cues about the words. Some dinosaur fanatics dig to find bones, others excavate to uncover fossil remains. Some pirates fight. Others face their foe brandishing a shimmering sword, commanding the land lubber (in their gruffest pirate impersonation) to walk the plank and become alligator stew. Give your child fertile soil on which to grow a rich vocabulary. Fill their imaginations with sights and sounds of curious places and people, and give them the words to express their visions. Read! When your voice gets tired, employ audiobooks.

Reading aloud gives the child an intuitive feel for sentence structure, grammar, and usage. A core piece of their education is exposure to these nuances of language.

Active listening and retelling a story (aka narration) is the cornerstone of the almighty reading comprehension skill that plagues so many! Modern Educators want to jump to *reading* comprehension without first mastering *listening* comprehension. I understand why. It's impossible to listen to 25 narrations in a single hour in a classroom. However, for a parent or a tutor, this is not only possible, it's easy and delightful. Try it. Read a very short story, maybe an Aesop's Fable. Then invite your child to tell it. Tell it to someone else. Pretend to be the characters and retell it together. Use puppets. Illustrate the scene. This skill of listening and retelling is vital!

Oral narration is not only the cornerstone of reading comprehension, but it's also the backbone of quality writing. Narrating the story helps the child in a myriad of ways, not the least of which is remembering the story for their own enjoyment. A child who narrates a story, is a child who can write that story once given the mechanical skills to do so. A child who narrates a story can bring the story into their pretend play and allow the author to breathe life into their own thoughts and ideas.

Beyond having a mind engaged in the story, a student must coordinate the eyes to see, the ears to hear, the voice to say, and the hand to write. This book is dedicated to *explicitly* building these sub-skills and *intentionally* coordinating them into fluid literacy. In my attempt to teach my own children, I've used several programs for teaching children to read, spell, and write. Each program that I've used comes with an assumption that the child will bring a natural ability to perform one or more of these sub-skills. Assumptions include either memorizing words on flashcards or learning to spell through rules will result in spontaneous reading, or immersion in quality books and copywork will lead to good spelling. While reading, spelling, and writing are interconnected skills and improvement in one area often does result in improvement in all areas, many children cannot make the leap from one into another without explicit teaching. It's my aim to provide parents and tutors with one reliable resource that assumes nothing upon the student, building each skill from the ground up. For that reason, I encourage youto complete every activity even if it seems too easy and especially if it seems too hard.

I must recognize *Word Mastery* by Florence Akin as the inspiration for the first several lessons in this book. I've not found a simpler method for introducing the 26 letters of the alphabet.

This book does not replace therapy provided by a professional. I encourage every parent who suspects dyslexia or a possible deficiency with speech, hearing, sight, or motor skills to get a professional evaluation and pursue all resources for helping your child.

Best wishes as you take a child on this exciting journey to literacy!

~Paula Van Kuren

Ground Rules

Temper your passionate desire for your student's success with compassionate understanding of your student's struggles. I firmly believe that every young child who grows up in a home where grown-ups read and write desire to read and write for themselves. The internal motivation is strong! If the reading or writing is not clicking, there is a struggle, a sub-skill that has not been learned fully. It's your job as a teacher to figure out where the struggle begins, and help your student overcome. Reading and writing are complex skills!

Limit lessons to 15 minutes. That is a maximum time limit. Go shorter if you have a wiggly youngster. Stop before anyone gets frustrated. A young child might only complete half of a page in 15 minutes. That's OK. An older child remediating a learning quirk may be able to get through a few pages in those same 15 minutes. Go at the student's pace. Don't rush. Don't push. Keep a positive atmosphere.

Do hard things, and do them well. Specifically, this program is designed to build up the sub-skills needed for fluent reading and writing. Each activity has a purpose towards that end. If you find a particular activity tiresome and difficult, it is likely because you have found *exactly* where your student struggles. *Move forward with compassionate determination.* Do not give into the temptation to skip the hard things. You will be skipping the exact thing your student needs the most! There is no rush! Take the time to build the foundation, even if it means taking your entire 15 minute lesson on one activity in the program. Stop for the day if you have reached the frustration point. Start again tomorrow.

The first time you see a new letter in this book, you are going to learn how to properly form the letter with verbal cues. Say the most common sound as you write or trace I'll explain that for each letter. as soon as formation is learned. Watch closely as your student writes each and every letter, and correct with a gentle reminder of the verbal cue before mistaken patterns are cemented.

I advise teaching the letter formation before meeting the letter in the Student Workbook. If you are working with an older student who already knows how to form letters well, this step is optional. If there is any hesitancy, do not skip this step however. If you are working with a very young child, consider saving the workbook lessons for a few months down the road, after a happy introduction to all the letters outside of workbooks (on a chalkboard or with magnets).

Choose from a list of gross-motor and sensory activities below. You should vary these activities from lesson to lesson to keep things fresh. If a letter is particularly troublesome, use several of these activities before trying the workbook pages. Some of these are geared towards young learners. Use your judgment to decide if a particular student will benefit from an activity. (Some 9 year olds enjoy fingerpaints. Others will view the activity as babyish.)

*   Chalkboard or white board: Write the letters as large as possible, using the entire arm to form the letter.

*   Sidewalk chalk: Write the letters as large as possible, using the entire arm to form the letter. You can make these into tracks for matchbox cars to race (in correct formation, of course), or make them so huge that your child can jump like a frog in letter formation (saying the sound of the letter instead of "ribbit").

*   Playdough: Roll out big snakes of playdough and form letters. Trace over them with the child's finger. Say the sounds as you finger trace.

*   Sandpaper letters: Trace over the letters with your child's pointer and middle fingers together, saying the formation first and then the letter sound.

*   Sandpaper Letters: Place paper over the letters and rub over with crayon. Use these crayon rubbings for future tracing practice.

*   Sandbox letters: Fill a flat box with ½ inch of sand (or salt). Use this sandbox to practice writing letters with a finger. Simply shake gently from side to side to erase. (A 13x9 plastic food storage dish works perfectly. It even has a good, tight lid for storage. A dark color is preferable in order to provide contrast between the sand & the box.)

*   Fingerpaint: Get the very large size painting paper and encourage your student to fill the page with a single letter (saying it's sound as you go), trace over the letter with a different color. Repeat as often as the child wishes. After the letter work, allow the child to free paint.

*   Fingertrace the letters on your student's back. Guess the letter. Now it's your turn to guess as your student traces a letter on your back. Try the same game on the palm of your hand. Close your eyes!

*   Air-write. Use the pointer-finger to "write" the letter in the air with large arm movements.

This list contains activities that are not directly letter learning They build the coordination and strength vital to reading and writing. If a child struggles to do several of these skills, it is likely that they will lack the coordination and upper body strength to succeed in their schoolwork. A child's play is their work. This work is vital. Don't hesitate to put the books down when attention wanes and go to the park.

* Monkey Bars

* Wheelbarrow races, push-ups, and any game that requires crawling.

* Riding a bicycle

* Swinging

* Running

* Skipping, hopping on one foot, jumping up high, jumping long

* Hopscotch

* Jump rope

* Ball games: catching, throwing, dribbling, kicking, etc.

* Martial Arts, Gymnastics, or Dance

* Cutting & pasting.

* Slicing soft foods with a blunt knife (banana). Spreading butter on bread. Spooning out cookie dough. Stirring ingredients.

* Wiping windows, tables, or floors with broad circular motion

* Sorting toys into bins and silverware in the drawer

* Playdoh

I recommend breaking chalk and crayons down to 1 inch nubs during the time period when your child is learning to form letters. This forces a tripod grasp. I'm also fond of triangular-shaped pencils and stetro grips for conventional pencils.

Colored pencils create a bright contrast between the white page and the child's own writing. That visual feedback facilitates learning. Don't be afraid to allow your child to use colored pencils. In fact, you can get more mileage out of the workbook pages if you encourage them to make a rainbow of each letter, repeating the tracing with multiple colors. Muscle-memory for letter formation is built with repetition. Make it colorful!

Auditory recognition is also built upon repetition. It helps the child to develop a sort of relationship with each letter. Once they have learned a letter in the Student Manual, place its magnet letter on the fridge. The whole family can cheer on the child's progress, and it's a frequent reminder to review the letters and their sounds. Make a game of rearranging the letters to make new words. Make up nonsense words, and then have fun making up a nonsense definition to your nonsense words.

Children's imaginations will be your best tutor!

Here is a sample lesson with instructions:

Cc

C   C   C

Instruct the student to trace the large letter, while you verbalize the strokes. For the letter C, "Start up high, curve around, stop." Try to stay within the lines.

Instruct the student to say the sound of the letter as he traces the 3 small letters.

(If you have used another handwriting curriculum, it's advisable to use previously taught cues for the strokes. These cues are a crutch that we are quick to outgrow, and not a central part of the lesson. I aim for simple. It is *not* simple to learn multiple cues for letter strokes. Whatever you have already taught is fine.)

It is vital for young learners to pull this part of the lesson off of the page. Practice the basic letters, their sounds and handwriting strokes, on a large chalkboard, outside with sidewalk chalk, in finger paints, in the sandbox with a stick, or even in the air using a finger as an imaginary marker. Use some sort of gross-motor activity with each letter because using the large muscles of the body, especially combined with say the sounds as you move, reinforces the letter in the child's memory. Once the letter strokes have become a part of the child's muscle-memory, you can drop the handwriting cues and the gross motor work.

As we introduce the basic 26 letters, we will give the student opportunity to brainstorm words that contain the sounds of the letters. Encourage your child to draw an object, cut & paste from a magazine, or stick a sticker on the page. Sometimes a word will have the same sound but use a different letter. (Kite and Cat) Help your child by saying, "You are right. That word does have the correct sound, but English is a funny language and we use a different letter to make that sound in that word." After all, learning that English is a "funny language" (with various patterns, exceptions and eccentricities) is a good rule of thumb to learn early. If we can make that idea a source of curiosity and challenge from the start, their minds will be prepared to tackle the hard work ahead.

You will notice that a child meets with different fonts for reading and writing in this book. The shape of the 'a' for example is different in book type than in D'Nealian Manuscript (a). I recommend using the flashcards at the end of the Teacher Manual to familiarize your child with various ways of shaping the letters. A basic game of Memory, matching the D'Nealian letters to the book type letters is easy and fun, and it works.

Circle c.

gjhcbhycdchujkclkghcascrqewrcbnjkccyutyfccrd

Underline from left to right with a colored pencil, looping the key letter as you go. Make certain to loop in the same motion as the cursive letter e. We are working on visual discrimination, line tracking, and handwriting motion in this activity.

tag   rag   fan   fat   met ◯

Use a cursor to uncover one sound at a time for each word. Then blend together the sounds in order to read the word. Many students will begin this process needing the tutor to verbalize the sounds before hearing the word. That's OK. There will be plenty of blending practice in this book. Give the help that your student needs today. If your student is able to say the sounds and blend the line without any help, draw eyes, nose, and a mouth in the circle to make a smiley face. If he requires help, draw only eyes. Go back through a 2nd time, and if he requires help again draw in the nose. Go back through a 3rd time and complete the smiley face with the mouth even if help is required. There is plenty of practice in this book. There is no need to grow frustrated. 3x and move along!

(Make a cursor by cutting a 2cm across/1cm down notch in a 3x5 index card. Use pastel colored cards if you can find them. Color contrast helps the eye, so long as it's not terribly bright.)

Ccc   *Sss*   *Eee*
Ttt   *Lll*   *Ggg*

The tutor will now dictate a *sound*. The student will identify the letter that makes the sound and trace the letter as they repeat the sound. Watch for proper letter formation. Dictate the sounds in the random order given.

L   S   E   T   C   G

C   E   L   T   S   G

S   G   C   L   E   T

cat

cat   cat   cat

Trace each letter as you say the sound. Try to stay within the lines. Can your student hear the word? /c/ /a/ /t/ = /cat/ You can help your student hear the blended word by finger tracing over the letters and saying the sounds. If your student still cannot hear the word, repeat and smoosh the sounds together more, making it easy to hear. Instruct your student to trace the word again 3 more times saying each individual sound and then blending the word.

The cat can play. The cat can sleep. I love the furry, soft cat.

Before you begin the sentence activity, ask your student to identify the key word (3x) by pointing with their finger (just like a word find puzzle). You are going to read these sentences aloud. As you read, your student is going to follow along and underline the sentences, looping the key word as you go (in the same motion of the cursive letter e). Stop the underline at the periods. Pick up the pencil. Continue the underlining new with each new sentence.

$$a\_ \quad m\_\_ \quad r\_\_$$
$$f \qquad n\_\_$$

Dictate each letter sound in random order. The student must identify the correct letter and repeat the sound as they trace. Then they write the letter on their own. You are watching for proper letter formation. Don't worry about sizing or spacing or neatness right now. Formation first. Some children cannot write independently while saying a sound. That's OK right now. Let them focus singularly on writing on the blank lines.

Mm   Sound /m/ as is moon.

~Capital *M*: Start at the top, down. Back to the top, down, up, down.

~~Lowercase m: Start at midline, down, bounce off baseline, hump, bounce, hump.

~~~At the bottom of the page is open space for drawing objects that contain a /m/ sound. (moon, money, monkey, mother, mud...)

~~~~Circle *m*.

Underline, starting at the left of the line, and loop each m as you move to the right. The loop must turn counter-clockwise, like a cursive e.

Aa   Sound /a/ as in apple.

~Capital *A*: Start at the top, slant to the left. Back to the top, slant to the right. Line through the middle, zip it up tight.

~~Lowercase *a*. Start at the midline, around the house, slide.

~~~At the bottom of the page is open space for drawing objects that contain a /a/ sound. (apple, ax, alligator, ant, Alabama)

~~~~Circle a.

Underline, starting at the left of the line, and loop each a as you move to the right. The loop must turn counter-clockwise, like a cursive e.

~~~~~Instruct your student to trace the sound you hear, repeating the sound as you trace. You are going to dictate each sound 3 times in the random order below. Watch for correct formation.

a   m   m   a   m   a

am

~Trace each letter and say its sound. Now, say each sound again. What word do you hear?

(Repeat this blending process, with more exaggerated pronunciation each time, if the child does not hear the word the first time.)

~~Now say "am" /a/ /m/ as you trace the word am 3x.

~~~Next, you will read a few sentences to your student. The student will underline the sentences as you read, looping the key word as the student moves from left to right.

~~~~If your student can write her name, let her write in on the blank line. If your student is still learning to write her name, write her name for her with a highlighter and allow her to trace the highlighted name.

Nn   Sound /n/ as in net.

~Capitol *N*:   Start at the top, down. Back to the top, down, up.

~~ Lowercase *n*:   Start at the midline, down, bounce off of baseline, hump.

~~~At the bottom of the page is open space for drawing objects that contain a /n/ sound. (net, new, next, number, ninja)

~~~~ Circle n.

> Underline, starting at the left of the line, and loop each *n* as you move to the right. The loop must turn counter-clockwise, like a cursive e.

~~~~~Instruct your student to trace the sound you hear, repeating the sound as you trace. You are going to dictate each sound 3 times in the random order below. Watch for correct formation.

n   a   m   m   n   a   a   m   n

man

~Trace each letter and say its sound. Now, say each sound again. What word do you hear?

(Repeat this blending process, with more exaggerated pronunciation each time, if the child does not hear the word the first time.)

~~Now say "man" /m/ /a/ /n/ as you trace the word 3x.

~~~Next, you will read a few sentences to your student. The student will underline the sentences as you read, looping the key word as the student moves from left to right.

~~~~ am   man   ○

Use a cursor to uncover one sound at a time. Instruct the student to say each sound as it is uncovered, then blend the sounds into the word. If your student is able to say the sounds and blend the line without any help, draw eyes, nose, and a mouth in the circle to make a smiley face. If he requires help, draw only eyes. Go back through a 2nd time, and if he requires help again draw in the nose. Go back through a 3rd time and complete the smiley face with the mouth even if help is required.

Rr   Sound /r/ as is red.

~Capitol *R*:   Start at the top, down. Back to the top, bubble, slide.

~~Lowercase *r*:   Start at the midline, down, bounce off of baseline, flag.

~~~At the bottom of the page is open space for drawing objects that contain a /r/ sound. (red, rug, run, rat, rest, rock)

~~~~Circle r.

Underline, starting at the left of the line, and loop each *r* as you move to the right. The loop must turn counter-clockwise, like a cursive e.

~~~~~Instruct your student to trace the sound you hear, repeating the sound as you trace. You are going to dictate each sound 3 times in the random order below. Watch for correct formation.

r   m   a   n   a   n   r   m   r   a   n   m

ran

~Trace each letter and say its sound. Now, say each sound again. What word do you hear?

(Repeat this blending process, with more exaggerated pronunciation each time, if the child does not hear the word the first time.)

~~Now say "ran" /r/ /a/ /n/ as you trace the word 3x.

~~~Next, you will read a few sentences to your student. The student will underline the sentences as you read, looping the key word as the student moves from left to right.

~~~~ man   am   ran   ◗

Use a cursor to uncover one sound at a time. Instruct the student to say each sound as it is uncovered, then blend the sounds into the word. If your student is able to say the sounds and blend the line without any help, draw eyes, nose, and a mouth in the circle to make a smiley face. If he requires help, draw only eyes. Go back through a 2nd time, and if he requires help again draw in the nose. Go back through a 3rd time and complete the smiley face with the mouth even if help is required.

Ff   Sound /f/ as is foot.

~Capitol *F*:   Start at the top, down. Back to the top, slide across. Midline, slide.

~~Lowercase *f*:   Start up high, swerve around, down. Cross at the midline

~~~At the bottom of the page is open space for drawing objects that contain a /f/ sound. (foot, food, fox, fall, friend)

~~~~Circle f.

> Underline, starting at the left of the line, and loop each f as you move to the right. The loop must turn counter-clockwise, like a cursive e.

~~~~~Instruct your student to trace the sound you hear, repeating the sound as you trace. You are going to dictate each sound 3 times in the random order below. Watch for correct formation.

a   r   f   m   n   f   m   r

a   a   n   r   f   m   n

fan

~Trace each letter and say its sound. Now, say each sound again. What word do you hear?

   (Repeat this blending process, with more exaggerated pronunciation each time, if the child does not hear the word the first time.)

~~Now say "fan" /f/ /a/ /n/ as you trace the word 3x.

~~~Next, you will read a few sentences to your student. The student will underline the sentences as you read, looping the key word as the student moves from left to right.

~~~~ am   man   fan   ran   ◯

    Use a cursor to uncover one sound at a time. Instruct the student to say each sound as it is uncovered, then blend the sounds into the word. If your student is able to say the sounds and blend the line without any help, draw eyes, nose, and a mouth in the circle to make a smiley face. If he requires help, draw only eyes. Go back through a 2nd time, and if he requires help again draw in the nose. Go back through a 3rd time and complete the smiley face with the mouth even if help is required.

Ss   Sound /s/ as in sock.

~Capitol *S*:   Start up high, ssslither left-right-left.

~~Lowercase *s*:   Start below the midline, ssslither left-right-left.

~~~At the bottom of the page is open space for drawing objects that contain a /s/ sound. (socks, sad, suit, sandbox, silly)

~~~~Circle s.

Underline, starting at the left of the line, and loop each s as you move to the right. The loop must turn counter-clockwise, like a cursive e.

~~~~~Instruct your student to trace the sound you hear, repeating the sound as you trace. You are going to dictate each sound 3 times in the random order below. Watch for correct formation.

n s f r m a m a s

r f n s r f m a n

Sam

~ Trace each letter and say its sound. Now, say each sound again. What word do you hear?

(Repeat this blending process, with more exaggerated pronunciation each time, if the child does not hear the word the first time.)

*Note that Sam is the name of a person. We capitalize the first letter of the names of people.

~~Now say "Sam" /s/ /a/ /m/ as you trace the word 3x.

~~~Next, you will read a few sentences to your student. The student will underline the sentences as you read, looping the key word as the student moves from left to right.

~~~~ Sam   man   fan   am   ran   ◯

Use a cursor to uncover one sound at a time. Instruct the student to say each sound as it is uncovered, then blend the sounds into the word. If your student is able to say the sounds and blend the line without any help, draw eyes, nose, and a mouth in the circle to make a smiley face. If he requires help, draw only eyes. Go back through a 2nd time, and if he requires help again draw in the nose. Go back through a 3rd time and complete the smiley face with the mouth even if help is required.

Ee   Sound /e/ as in elephant.

~Capitol *E*:   Start at the top, slide left, down, slide right. Back to midline, slide right.

~~Lowercase *e*:   Start low, loop around.

~~~At the bottom of the page is open space for drawing objects that contain a /e/ sound. (elephant, elf, envelope, empty, egg)

~~~~Circle e.

Underline, starting at the left of the line, and loop each e as you move to the right. The loop must turn counter-clockwise, like a cursive e.

~~~~~Instruct your student to trace the sound you hear, repeating the sound as you trace. You are going to dictate each sound 3 times in the random order below. Watch for correct formation.

r f n s r f e a n

n s f r e a e a s

men

~Trace each letter and say its sound. Now, say each sound again. What word do you hear?

(Repeat this blending process, with more exaggerated pronunciation each time, if the child does not hear the word the first time.)

~~Now say "men" /m/ /e/ /n/ as you trace the word 3x.

~~~Next, you will read a few sentences to your student. The student will underline the sentences as you read, looping the key word as the student moves from left to right.

~~~~ men   man   fan   Sam   ran ◯

Use a cursor to uncover one sound at a time. Instruct the student to say each sound as it is uncovered, then blend the sounds into the word. If your student is able to say the sounds and blend the line without any help, draw eyes, nose, and a mouth in the circle to make a smiley face. If he requires help, draw only eyes. Go back through a 2nd time, and if he requires help again draw in the nose. Go back through a 3rd time and complete the smiley face with the mouth even if help is required.

Tt   Sound /t/ as in time.

~Capitol *T*:   Start at the top, down. Cross at the top.

~~Lowercase *t*:   Start up high, down with a connector. Cross at the midline.

~~~ At the bottom of the page is open space for drawing objects that contain a /e/ sound. (elephant, elf, envelope, empty, egg)

~~~~Circle t.

Underline, starting at the left of the line, and loop each t as you move to the right. The loop must turn counter-clockwise, like a cursive e.

~~~~~Instruct your student to trace the sound you hear, repeating the sound as you trace. You are going to dictate each sound 3 times in the random order below. Watch for correct formation.

r   f   n   s   r   f   e   t   n

n   s   f   r   e   t   e   t   s

ten

~Trace each letter and say its sound. Now, say each sound again. What word do you hear?

   (Repeat this blending process, with more exaggerated pronunciation each time, if the child does not hear the word the first time.)

~~Now say "ten" /t/ /e/ /n/ as you trace the word 3x.

~~~ Next, you will read a few sentences to your student. The student will underline the sentences as you read, looping the key word as the student moves from left to right.

~~~~ Say the sound, trace. Write the letter. Repeat for each letter.

~~~~~Use a cursor to practice reading.

Ll   Sound /l/ as in lion.

~Capitol *L*:   Start at the top, down, slide.

~~Lowercase *l*:   Start at the top, down with connector.

~~~At the bottom of the page is open space for drawing objects that contain a /l/ sound. (lion, lollipop, lemon, laugh)

~~~~Circle l.

Underline, starting at the left of the line, and loop each l as you move to the right. The loop must turn counter-clockwise, like a cursive e.

~~~~~Instruct your student to trace the sound you hear, repeating the sound as you trace. You are going to dictate each sound 3 times in the random order below. Watch for correct formation.

r f t s r f e l t

t s f r e l e l s

let

~ Trace each letter and say its sound. Now, say each sound again. What word do you hear?

   (Repeat this blending process, with more exaggerated pronunciation each time, if the child does not hear the word the first time.)

~~ Now say "let" /l/ /e/ /t/ as you trace the word 3x.

~~~Next, you will read a few sentences to your student. The student will underline the sentences as you read, looping the key word as the student moves from left to right.

~~~~Say the sound, trace. Write the letter. Repeat for each letter.

~~~~~Use a cursor to practice reading.

Gg   Sound /g/ as in green.

~Capitol G: Start up high, curve around to the midline, slide.

~~Lowercase *g*:   Start at the midline, all the way around, down for a tail.

~~~At the bottom of the page is open space for drawing objects that contain a /l/ sound. (green, gum, gas, garage, garbage)

~~~~Circle g.

~~~~~Use cursor to practice reading.

~~~~~~Instruct your student to trace the sound you hear, repeating the sound as you trace. You are going to dictate each sound 3 times in the random order below. Watch for correct formation.

g f t s g f e l t

t s f g e l e l s

gas

~ Trace each letter and say its sound. Now, say each sound again. What word do you hear?

   (Repeat this blending process, with more exaggerated pronunciation each time, if the child does not hear the word the first time.)

~~ Now say "gas" /g/ /a/ /s/ as you trace the word 3x.

~~~ Next, you will read a few sentences to your student. The student will underline the sentences as you read, looping the key word as the student moves from left to right.

~~~~Say the sound, trace. Write the letter. Repeat for each letter.

   a   *r*   *m*   *n*___

~~~~~Use a cursor to practice reading.

Cc   Sound /c/ as in cat.

~Capitol *C*:   Start up high, curve around, stop.

~~ Lowercase *c*:   Start below the midline, curve around, stop.

~~~At the bottom of the page is open space for drawing objects that contain a /c/ sound. (cat, coin, carpet, car, cabin)

~~~~Circle c.

~~~~~Use cursor to practice reading.

~~~~~~Instruct your student to trace the sound you hear, repeating the sound as you trace. You are going to dictate each sound 3 times in the random order below. Watch for correct formation.

c g t s c g e l t

t s g c e l e l s

cat

~Trace each letter and say its sound. Now, say each sound again. What word do you hear?

(Repeat this blending process, with more exaggerated pronunciation each time, if the child does not hear the word the first time.)

~~ Now say "cat" /c/ /a/ /t/ as you trace the word 3x.

~~~Next, you will read a few sentences to your student. The student will underline the sentences as you read, looping the key word as the student moves from left to right.

~~~~Say the sound, trace. Write the letter. Repeat for each letter.

a__ m__ r__

f__ n__

~~~~~Use a cursor to practice reading.

Page 23

Bb   Sound /b/ as in bubble.

~Capitol *B*:   Start at the top, down. Back to the top, bubble, bubble.

~~Lowercase *b*:   Start at the top, down. Back to the midline, bubble.

~~~At the bottom of the page is open space for drawing objects that contain a /b/ sound. (bubble, bat, box, blue)

~~~~Circle b.

~~~~~Use a cursor to practice reading.

~~~~~~Instruct your student to trace the sound you hear, repeating the sound as you trace. You are going to dictate each sound 3 times in the random order below. Watch for correct formation.

c b t g c b e l t

t g b c e l e l g

bat

~Trace each letter and say its sound. Now, say each sound again. What word do you hear?

(Repeat this blending process, with more exaggerated pronunciation each time, if the child does not hear the word the first time.)

~~Now say "bat" /b/ /a/ /t/ as you trace the word 3x.

~~~Next, you will read a few sentences to your student. The student will underline the sentences as you read, looping the key word as the student moves from left to right.

*Notice that we added an s to 'bat' in the last sentence because we are talking about many bats, not just one.

~~~~Say the sound, trace. Write the letter. Repeat for each letter.

*m_ a_ f_ r_*

*s_ n_*

~~~~~Use a cursor to practice reading.

Ii   Sound /i/ as in inside.

~Capitol *I*:   Start at the top, down, slide up high, slide down low.

~~ Lowercase *i*:   Start at the midline, down with a connector, dot.

~~~At the bottom of the page is open space for drawing objects that contain a /i/ sound. (inside, igloo, icky)

~~~~Circle i.

~~~~~Use the cursor to practice reading.

~~~~~~Instruct your student to trace the sound you hear, repeating the sound as you trace. You are going to dictate each sound 3 times in the random order below. Watch for correct formation.

I b l t c i g b t

g l b i t i c g c

it

~Trace each letter and say its sound. Now, say each sound again. What word do you hear?

(Repeat this blending process, with more exaggerated pronunciation each time, if the child does not hear the word the first time.)

~~ Now say "it" /i/ /t/ as you trace the word 3x.

~~~ Next, you will read a few sentences to your student. The student will underline the sentences as you read, looping the key word as the student moves from left to right.

~~~~Say the sound, trace. Write the letter. Repeat for each letter.

m   e   s   f   r

a   n

~~~~~Use a cursor to practice reading.

Kk   Sound /k/ as in kite.

~Capitol *K*:   Start at the top, down. Top, slant, hit, swerve.

~~Lowercase *k*:   Start at the top, down, back to the midline, petal, swerve.

~~~At the bottom of the page is open space for drawing objects that contain a /k/ sound. (kite, kitten, kit, kid)

~~~~Circle k.

~~~~~Use the cursor to practice reading.

~~~~~~Instruct your student to trace the sound you hear, repeating the sound as you trace. You are going to dictate each sound 3 times in the random order below. Watch for correct formation.

c   i   b   k   c   i   g   l   b

b   k   i   c   g   l   g   l   k

kit

~Trace each letter and say its sound. Now, say each sound again. What word do you hear?

(Repeat this blending process, with more exaggerated pronunciation each time, if the child does not hear the word the first time.)

~~Now say "kit" /k/ /i/ /t/ as you trace the word 3x.

~~~Next, you will read a few sentences to your student. The student will underline the sentences as you read, looping the key word as the student moves from left to right.

~~~~Say the sound, trace. Write the letter. Repeat for each letter.

m   e_   s_   f_   r__

t_   a_   n__

~~~~~Use a cursor to practice reading.

Page 29

Hh Sound /h/ as in hat.

~Capitol *H*: Start at the top, down. Start at the top, down. Slide at the midline.

~~Lowercase *h*: Start at the top, down, back to the midline,hump.

~~~At the bottom of the page (and in the margins) is open space for drawing objects that contain a /h/ sound. (hat, head, hop, happy, hero)

~~~~ Circle h.

~~~~~Use the cursor to practice reading.

~~~~~~Instruct your student to trace the sound you hear, repeating the sound as you trace. You are going to dictate each sound 3 times in the random order below. Watch for correct formation.

c i b k c i g h b

b k i c g h g h k

hat

~Trace each letter and say its sound. Now, say each sound again. What word do you hear?

(Repeat this blending process, with more exaggerated pronunciation each time, if the child does not hear the word the first time.)

~~Now say "hat" /h/ /a/ /t/ as you trace the word 3x.

~~~Next, you will read a few sentences to your student. The student will underline the sentences as you read, looping the key word as the student moves from left to right.

~~~~Say the sound, trace. Write the letter. Repeat for each letter.

*m   e_   s_   f_   r_*

*g_   t_   a_   n_*

~~~~~Use a cursor to practice reading.

Dd   Sound /d/ as in dog.

~Capitol *D*:   Start at the top, down. Back to the top, drive around and down.

~~Lowercase *d*:   Start at the midline, around, all the way up and down with a connector.

~~~At the bottom of the page is open space for drawing objects that contain a /d/ sound. (dog, dig, dirt, Dad, drive)

~~~~Circle d.

~~~~~Use the cursor to practice reading.

~~~~~~Instruct your student to trace the sound you hear, repeating the sound as you trace. You are going to dictate each sound 3 times in the random order below. Watch for correct formation.

d h b k d c i h b

b k d i c h k c i

dig

~Trace each letter and say its sound. Now, say each sound again. What word do you hear?

(Repeat this blending process, with more exaggerated pronunciation each time, if the child does not hear the word the first time.)

~~ Now say "dig" /d/ /i/ /g/ as you trace the word 3x.

~~~Next, you will read a few sentences to your student. The student will underline the sentences as you read, looping the key word as the student moves from left to right.

~~~~Say the sound, trace. Write the letter. Repeat for each letter.

m   e__   s__   f__   r__

a__   n__   c__   t__   g__

~~~~~Use a cursor to practice reading.

Pp   Sound /p/ as in pig.

~Capitol *P*:   Start at the top, down. Back to the top, just one bubble.

~~Lowercase *p*:   Start at the midline, down so low. Back to the midline, just one bubble.

~~~At the bottom of the page is open space for drawing objects that contain a /p/ sound. (pig, park, point, princess, prince, popcorn)

~~~~ Circle p.

~~~~~Use the cursor to practice reading.

~~~~~~Instruct your student to trace the sound you hear, repeating the sound as you trace. You are going to dictate each sound 3 times in the random order below. Watch for correct formation.

d h b k d p i h b

b k d i p h k p i

pig

~Trace each letter and say its sound. Now, say each sound again. What word do you hear?

(Repeat this blending process, with more exaggerated pronunciation each time, if the child does not hear the word the first time.)

~~Now say "pig" /p/ /i/ /g/ as you trace the word 3x.

~~~Next, you will read a few sentences to your student. The student will underline the sentences as you read, looping the key word as the student moves from left to right.

~~~~Say the sound, trace. Write the letter. Repeat for each letter.

b   e_   s_   f_   r__

a_   n_   c_   t_   g__

~~~~~Use a cursor to practice reading.

Oo   Sound /o/ as in octopus.

~Capitol *O*:   Start at the top, circle all the way around.

~~ Lowercase *o*:   Start at the midline, circle all the way around.

~~~At the bottom of the page is open space for drawing objects that contain a /o/ sound. (octopus, ox, octagon, olive, on, off)

~~~~Circle o.

~~~~~Use the cursor to practice reading.

~~~~~~ Instruct your student to trace the sound you hear, repeating the sound as you trace. You are going to dictate each sound 3 times in the random order below. Watch for correct formation.

d h p k d o i h p

o k d i p h k o i

off

~ Trace each letter and say its sound. Now, say each sound again. What word do you hear?

(Repeat this blending process, with more exaggerated pronunciation each time, if the child does not hear the word the first time.)

~~Now say "off" /o/ /ff/ as you trace the word 3x.

~~~Next, you will read a few sentences to your student. The student will underline the sentences as you read, looping the key word as the student moves from left to right.

~~~~Say the sound, trace. Write the letter. Repeat for each letter.

b e_ s_ f_ r_

i_ n_ c_ t_ g_

~~~~~Use a cursor to practice reading.

Jj   Sound /j/ as in jug.

~Capitol *J*:   Start at the top, down with a tail.

~~ Lowercase *j*:   Start at the midline, down low with a tail. Dot.

~~~ At the bottom of the page is open space for drawing objects that contain a /j/ sound. (jug, jump, jam, Jupiter)

~~~~Circle j.

~~~~~Use the cursor to practice reading.

~~~~~~ Instruct your student to trace the sound you hear, repeating the sound as you trace. You are going to dictate each sound 3 times in the random order below. Watch for correct formation.

d h j k d p o h j

j k d o p h k p o

jet

~ Trace each letter and say its sound. Now, say each sound again. What word do you hear?

(Repeat this blending process, with more exaggerated pronunciation each time, if the child does not hear the word the first time.)

~~Now say "jet" /j/ /e/ /t/ as you trace the word 3x.

~~~Next, you will read a few sentences to your student. The student will underline the sentences as you read, looping the key word as the student moves from left to right.

~~~~Say the sound, trace. Write the letter. Repeat for each letter.

b   e_   s_   f_   r_

i_   m_   c   t_   g_

~~~~~Use a cursor to practice reading.

Ww   Sound /w/ as in wind.

~ Capitol *W*:   Start at the top, down, up, down, up.

~~Lowercase *w*: Start at the midline, down, up, down, up.

~~~At the bottom of the page is open space for drawing objects that contain a /w/ sound. (wig, wind, water, wish, web)

~~~~Circle w.

~~~~~Use the cursor to practice reading.

~~~~~~Instruct your student to trace the sound you hear, repeating the sound as you trace. You are going to dictate each sound 3 times in the random order below. Watch for correct formation.

d h j w d p o h j

j w d o p h w p o

web

~ Trace each letter and say its sound. Now, say each sound again. What word do you hear?

  (Repeat this blending process, with more exaggerated pronunciation each time, if the child does not hear the word the first time.)

~~Now say "web" /w/ /e/ /b/ as you trace the word 3x.

~~~Next, you will read a few sentences to your student. The student will underline the sentences as you read, looping the key word as the student moves from left to right.

~~~~Say the sound, trace. Write the letter. Repeat for each letter.

b   e_   s__   h__   k__

i_   a_   c   t_   g_

~~~~~Use a cursor to practice reading.

Uu   Sound /u/ as in umbrella.

~Capitol *U*:   Start at the top, down and up, down with a connector.

~~Lowercase *u*:   Start at the midline, down and up, down with a connector.

~~~At the bottom of the page is open space for drawing objects that contain a /u/ sound. (umbrella, up, under,)

~~~~Circle u.

~~~~~Use the cursor to practice reading.

~~~~~~Instruct your student to trace the sound you hear, repeating the sound as you trace. You are going to dictate each sound 3 times in the random order below. Watch for correct formation.

d w j u d p o w j

j u d o p w u p o

up

~Trace each letter and say its sound. Now, say each sound again. What word do you hear?

(Repeat this blending process, with more exaggerated pronunciation each time, if the child does not hear the word the first time.)

~~Now say "up" /u/ /p/ as you trace the word 3x.

~~~Next, you will read a few sentences to your student. The student will underline the sentences as you read, looping the key word as the student moves from left to right.

~~~~Say the sound, trace. Write the letter. Repeat for each letter.

c_ e_ b_ k_ n_

g_ t_ i_ h_ d_

~~~~~Use a cursor to practice reading.

Zz   Sound /z/ as in zipper.

~Capitol *Z*:   Start at the top, slide, down, slide.

~~Lowercase *z*:   Start at the midline, slide, down, slide.

~~~At the bottom of the page is open space for drawing objects that contain a /z/ sound. (zipper, zebra, zap)

~~~~Circle z.

~~~~~Use the cursor to practice reading.

~~~~~~Instruct your student to trace the sound you hear, repeating the sound as you trace. You are going to dictate each sound 3 times in the random order below. Watch for correct formation.

z   w   j   u   z   p   o   w   j

j   u   z   o   p   w   u   p   o

zip

~Trace each letter and say its sound. Now, say each sound again. What word do you hear?

(Repeat this blending process, with more exaggerated pronunciation each time, if the child does not hear the word the first time.)

~~Now say "zip" /z/ /i/ /p/ as you trace the word 3x.

~~~ Next, you will read a few sentences to your student. The student will underline the sentences as you read, looping the key word as the student moves from left to right.

~~~~Say the sound, trace. Write the letter. Repeat for each letter.

c__ p__ b__ k__ r__

g__ t__ i__ h__ d__

~~~~~Use a cursor to practice reading.

Xx   Sound /x/ as in the end of box.

~Capitol *X*:   Start at the top, slide and swerve. Back to the top, diagonal down.

~~ Lowercase *x*:   Start at the midline, slide and swerve. Back to the top, diagonal down.

~~~At the bottom of the page is open space for drawing objects that contain a /x/ sound. (box, fox, ax, ox, fix, mix)

~~~~Circle x.

~~~~~Use the cursor to practice reading.

~~~~~~Instruct your student to trace the sound you hear, repeating the sound as you trace. You are going to dictate each sound 3 times in the random order below. Watch for correct formation.

z   w   j   u   z   x   o   w   j

j   u   z   o   x   w   u   x   o

box

~Trace each letter and say its sound. Now, say each sound again. What word do you hear?

   (Repeat this blending process, with more exaggerated pronunciation each time, if the child does not hear the word the first time.)

~~Now say "box" /b/ /o/ /x/ as you trace the word 3x.

~~~Next, you will read a few sentences to your student. The student will underline the sentences as you read, looping the key word as the student moves from left to right.

~~~~ Say the sound, trace. Write the letter. Repeat for each letter.

c__ p b__ k__ o

g f i h d__

~~~~~Use a cursor to practice reading.

Vv   Sound /v/ as in van.

~Capitol *V*:   Start at the top, down, up.

~~Lowercase *v*:   Start at the midline, down, up.

~~~At the bottom of the page is open space for drawing objects that contain a /v/ sound. (van, vehicle, viper, volume)

~~~~Circle v.

~~~~~Use the cursor to practice reading.

~~~~~~Instruct your student to trace the sound you hear, repeating the sound as you trace. You are going to dictate each sound 3 times in the random order below. Watch for correct formation.

x w j u x v z w j

j u z x v w u v z

van

~Trace each letter and say its sound. Now, say each sound again. What word do you hear?

(Repeat this blending process, with more exaggerated pronunciation each time, if the child does not hear the word the first time.)

~~Now say "van" /v/ /a/ /n/ as you trace the word 3x.

~~~Next, you will read a few sentences to your student. The student will underline the sentences as you read, looping the key word as the student moves from left to right.

~~~~ Say the sound, trace. Write the letter. Repeat for each letter.

c__ p b__ k__ o
j s i h d__

~~~~~Use a cursor to practice reading.

Page 49

Yy   Sound /y/ as in yellow.

~Capitol *Y*:   Start at the top, slide down to the midline. Back to the top, down on a diagonal.

~~Lowercase *y*:   Start at the midline, down, up, down with a tail.

~~~At the bottom of the page is open space for drawing objects that contain a /y/ sound. (yellow, yard, yarn, yes, yogurt)

~~~~Circle y.

~~~~~Use the cursor to practice reading.

~~~~~~Instruct your student to trace the sound you hear, repeating the sound as you trace. You are going to dictate each sound 3 times in the random order below. Watch for correct formation.

z w y u z x v w y

y u z v x w u x v

yes

~Trace each letter and say its sound. Now, say each sound again. What word do you hear?

(Repeat this blending process, with more exaggerated pronunciation each time, if the child does not hear the word the first time.)

~~Now say "yes" /y/ /e/ /s/ as you trace the word 3x.

~~~Next, you will read a few sentences to your student. The student will underline the sentences as you read, looping the key word as the student moves from left to right.

~~~~ Say the sound, trace. Write the letter. Repeat for each letter.

j_ p_ b_ k_ o_
w_ e_ i_ h_ d_

~~~~~Use a cursor to practice reading.

Qu qu   Sound /qu/ as in quiet.

Note: In English, Q is always accompanied by u.

~Capitol *Q*:   Start at the top, go all the way around. Make a swerve at the baseline.

~~Lowercase *q*:   Start at the midline, go all the way around, down with a backwards tail. *Note: Sometimes q simply has a straight line down past the baseline instead of the backwards tail.*

~~~At the bottom of the page is open space for drawing objects that contain a /qu/ sound. (quiet, quack, quake, quail, quit)

~~~~Circle q.

~~~~~Use the cursor to practice reading.

~~~~~~ Instruct your student to trace the sound you hear, repeating the sound as you trace. You are going to dictate each sound 3 times in the random order below. Watch for correct formation.

z   qu   x   z   v   y   qu

z   y   x   v   qu   v   y   x

quit

~Trace each letter and say its sound. Now, say each sound again. What word do you hear?

(Repeat this blending process, with more exaggerated pronunciation each time, if the child does not hear the word the first time.)

~~Now say "quit" /qu/ /i/ /t/ as you trace the word 3x.

~~~Next, you will read a few sentences to your student. The student will underline the sentences as you read, looping the key word as the student moves from left to right.

~~~~ Say the sound, trace. Write the letter. Repeat for each letter.

j   p_   w_   k_   o_
u_   t_   i_   h_   d_

~~~~~Use a cursor to practice reading.

The next section of lessons will build upon the knowledge of the 26 letters. If your student is unsure of any letter, take the time now to review before moving forward.

Now the letters are familiar, so we can talk about different ways in which they work. First, we will introduce the concept of vowels and consonants. The vowels are 'a-e-i-o-u and sometimes y' (but we aren't going to let 'y' play with the other vowels today).

Use letter flashcards to illustrate each letter as you work through the next activities.

Open your mouth and put two fingers inside. Don't let your lips, teeth, or tongue touch your fingers. Now, say the vowels "a-e-i-o-u." Can you do it? Now go through each individual vowel and prove that they can be sounded without touching. This is a good time to review the letter sounds as well as teach the vowel/consonant concept.

Now try it with some other letters (b, p, t, k...). Those other letters are consonants, and we cannot say them with our fingers in our mouths because we must use our lips and tongue and teeth to say them.

*Vowels usually say either their name or their short sound. (O can also say /oo/ as in do and to. A can say /ah/ as in all and ma. But we don't want to overwhelm with too many details, so teach those sounds only as they come apparent in words.)

*Vowels usually say their short sound when they are between two consonants. We call this a closed syllable because the consonant at the end is like a door that closes the vowel inside.

Next, ask your student to listen for the vowel sound in each word as you say it aloud, and hold up the vowel flashcard that makes that sound.

bat	hot	rub	bell	hid
hug	wig	rat	hog	hen

Page 53

~Instruct your student to write their name on the line. If this is a struggle, write their name with a highlighter and let them trace over the highlighted name.

~~Lay the vowel flashcards in a row in front of the student, above their workbook and in a-e-i-o-u order. You are going to say a vowel sound. Ask the student point to the letter that makes that sound, and then trace/write the letter in the student workbook.

a	e	i	o	u
i	o	a	e	u
e	u	o	i	a

~~~Use the cursor to uncover one sound at a time to read the review words. Mark as completed as in previous lessons.

~~~~Ask the student to say the sound of each letter as they trace and then copy each letter.

Page 54

~Dictate a sound for your student to trace.

m	y	v	qu	x	z
z	qu	m	x	y	v
qu	v	x	m	y	z

~~Use the cursor to read the practice words. Notice the third line is a sentence. We begin a sentence with a capital letter and end it with a period.

~~~Instruct the student to read each word, sound by sound, using a cursor if needed. Then trace as they break the word apart into sounds again.

~~~~Next, you will read a few sentences to your student. The student will underline the sentences as you read, looping the key word as the student moves from left to right.

Page 55

~Instruct your student to write their name on the line. If this is a struggle, write their name with a highlighter and let them trace over the highlighted name.

~~Lay the vowel flashcards in a row in front of the student, above their workbook and in a-e-i-o-u order. You are going to say a vowel sound. Ask the student point to the letter that makes that sound, and then trace/write the letter in the student workbook.

a	e	i	o	u
e	u	o	i	a
i	o	a	e	u

~~~Use the cursor to uncover one sound at a time to read the review words. Mark as completed as in previous lessons.

~~~~Ask the student to say the sound of each letter as they trace and then copy each letter.

Page 56

~Dictate a sound for your student to trace.

v	a	y	qu	m	x
x	a	m	y	qu	v
qu	y	m	x	a	v

~~Use the cursor to read the practice words. Notice the third line is a sentence. We begin a sentence with a capital letter and end it with a period.

~~~Instruct the student to read each word, sound by sound, using a cursor if needed. Then trace as they break the word apart into sounds again.

~~~~Next, you will read a few sentences to your student. The student will underline the sentences as you read, looping the key word as the student moves from left to right.

~Instruct your student to write their name on the line. If this is a struggle, write their name with a highlighter and let them trace over the highlighted name.

~~Lay the vowel flashcards in a row in front of the student, above their workbook and in a-e-i-o-u order. You are going to say a vowel sound. Ask the student point to the letter that makes that sound, and then trace/write the letter in the student workbook.

a	e	i	o	u
a	i	o	e	u
o	e	u	i	a

~~~Use the cursor to uncover one sound at a time to read the review words. Mark as completed as in previous lessons.

~~~~Ask the student to say the sound of each letter as they trace and then copy each letter.

Page 58

~Dictate a sound for your student to trace.

y	a	m	qu	v	n
m	n	qu	a	y	v
n	a	m	v	qu	y

~~Use the cursor to read the practice words. Notice the third line is a sentence. We begin a sentence with a capital letter and end it with a period.

~~~Instruct the student to read each word, sound by sound, using a cursor if needed. Then trace as they break the word apart into sounds again.

~~~~Next, you will read a few sentences to your student. The student will underline the sentences as you read, looping the key word as the student moves from left to right.

~Instruct your student to write their name on the line. If this is a struggle, write their name with a highlighter and let them trace over the highlighted name.

~~Lay the vowel flashcards in a row in front of the student, above their workbook and in a-e-i-o-u order. You are going to say a vowel sound. Ask the student point to the letter that makes that sound, and then trace/write the letter in the student workbook.

a	e	i	o	u
e	u	i	o	u
o	i	a	a	e

~~~Use the cursor to uncover one sound at a time to read the review words. Mark as completed as in previous lessons.

~~~~Ask the student to say the sound of each letter as they trace and then copy each letter.

Page 60

~Dictate a sound for your student to trace.

r	a	n	m	qu	v
a	m	v	qu	n	r
v	n	m	qu	r	a

~~Use the cursor to read the practice words. Notice the third line is a sentence. We begin a sentence with a capital letter and end it with a period.

~~~Instruct the student to read each word, sound by sound, using a cursor if needed. Then trace as they break the word apart into sounds again.

~~~~Next, you will read a few sentences to your student. The student will underline the sentences as you read, looping the key word as the student moves from left to right.

Page 61

~Instruct your student to write their name on the line. If this is a struggle, write their name with a highlighter and let them trace over the highlighted name.

~~Lay the vowel flashcards in a row in front of the student, above their workbook and in a-e-i-o-u order. You are going to say a vowel sound. Ask the student point to the letter that makes that sound, and then trace/write the letter in the student workbook.

u	o	e	a	i
i	o	a	e	u
e	u	o	i	a

~~~Use the cursor to uncover one sound at a time to read the review words. Mark as completed as in previous lessons.

~~~~Ask the student to say the sound of each letter as they trace and then copy each letter.

Page 62

~Dictate a sound for your student to trace.

f	qu	a	r	n	m
r	f	n	a	qu	m
m	qu	a	f	n	r

~~Use the cursor to read the practice words. Notice the third line is a sentence. We begin a sentence with a capital letter and end it with a period.

~~~Instruct the student to read each word, sound by sound, using a cursor if needed. Then trace as they break the word apart into sounds again.

~~~~Next, you will read a few sentences to your student. The student will underline the sentences as you read, looping the key word as the student moves from left to right.

Page 63

~Instruct your student to write their name on the line. If this is a struggle, write their name with a highlighter and let them trace over the highlighted name.

~~Lay the vowel flashcards in a row in front of the student, above their workbook and in a-e-i-o-u order. You are going to say a vowel sound. Ask the student point to the letter that makes that sound, and then trace/write the letter in the student workbook.

e	u	o	i	a
o	u	a	e	i
i	o	a	e	u

~~~Use the cursor to uncover one sound at a time to read the review words. Mark as completed as in previous lessons.

~~~~Ask the student to say the sound of each letter as they trace and then copy each letter.

~Dictate a sound for your student to trace.

r	s	f	n	m	a
s	n	a	m	f	r
n	m	a	s	r	f

~~Use the cursor to read the practice words. Notice the third line is a sentence. We begin a sentence with a capital letter and end it with a period.

~~~Instruct the student to read each word, sound by sound, using a cursor if needed. Then trace as they break the word apart into sounds again.

~~~~Next, you will read a few sentences to your student. The student will underline the sentences as you read, looping the key word as the student moves from left to right.

Page 65

~Instruct your student to write their name on the line. If this is a struggle, write their name with a highlighter and let them trace over the highlighted name.

~~Lay the vowel flashcards in a row in front of the student, above their workbook and in a-e-i-o-u order. You are going to say a vowel sound. Ask the student point to the letter that makes that sound, and then trace/write the letter in the student workbook.

i	o	o	i	a
a	e	u	e	u
u	o	a	e	i

~~~Use the cursor to uncover one sound at a time to read the review words. Mark as completed as in previous lessons.

~~~~Ask the student to say the sound of each letter as they trace and then copy each letter.

Page 66

~Dictate a sound for your student to trace.

f	e	s	n	a	r
r	s	e	n	a	f
e	s	a	f	r	n

~~Use the cursor to read the practice words. Notice the third line is a sentence. We begin a sentence with a capital letter and end it with a period.

~~~Instruct the student to read each word, sound by sound, using a cursor if needed. Then trace as they break the word apart into sounds again.

~~~~Next, you will read a few sentences to your student. The student will underline the sentences as you read, looping the key word as the student moves from left to right.

Placement Test

Page 67

Placement Test

Instruct your student to trace each letter as they say the sound that it makes. Then copy.

Read through each word with a cursor. Three helps are allowed. If student needs more than three helps on the whole page, go back and redo pages 53-67

~Dictate the words below. Ask your student to listen for the vowel sound in the middle of the word (/a/ in cat, for example). If they cannot hear the sound, help them by repeating the word and slowly breaking apart the sounds as you speak. (/c/ /a/ /t/) Trace or copy the vowel that is heard in the word.

cat	met	pit	top	cup
fell	hot	hit	fan	sun
did	wax	gut	red	hop

~~Use the cursor to read the practice words.

~~~Instruct your student to say the sound of the letter as they trace each letter. Then copy.

* Vowels can say their name at the end of a syllable. Sometimes an 'o' at the end of a syllable says /oo/ as in to and do.

~Dictate the words below. Ask your student to say each sound as they trace the word that they hear.

> I   go   we   a   me

~~Use the cursor to read the practice sentences.

~~~Dictate a sound for your student to trace.

e	t	s	f	n	r
n	s	r	f	e	t
t	s	f	e	r	n

~~~Next, you will read a few sentences to your student. The student will underline the sentences as you read, looping the key word as the student moves from left to right.

~Dictate the words below. Ask your student to listen for the vowel sound in the middle of the word (/a/ in cat, for example). If they cannot hear the sound, help them by repeating the word and slowly breaking apart the sounds as you speak. (/c/ /a/ /t/) Trace or copy the vowel that is heard in the word.

ran	dog	pup	bell	hill
mud	mad	fed	sick	pop
beg	bag	big	bog	bug

~~Use the cursor to read the practice words.

~~~Instruct your student to say the sound of the letter as they trace each letter. Then copy.

~Dictate the words below. Ask your student to say each sound as they trace the word that they hear.

      so   be   he   no   me

~~Use the cursor to read the practice sentences.

~~~Dictate a sound for your student to trace.

r	t	l	f	e	s
s	t	l	f	r	e
l	e	r	t	s	f

~~~~Next, you will read a few sentences to your student. The student will underline the sentences as you read, looping the key word as the student moves from left to right.

~Dictate the words below. Ask your student to say each sound as they trace the word that they hear.

I me we so to go

~~Use the cursor to read the practice words.

~ Dictate a sound for your student to trace.

e	s	l	t	g	f
g	l	t	e	s	f
f	g	s	e	l	t

~~ Use the cursor to read the practice sentences.

~~~ Trace and copy each letter as you say its sound.

~~~~Next, you will read a few sentences to your student. The student will underline the sentences as you read, looping the key word as the student moves from left to right.

~Dictate the words below. Ask your student to say each sound as they trace the word that they hear.

be   he   me   to   no

~~Use the cursor to read the practice words.

~ Dictate a sound for your student to trace.

g	c	l	f	e	t
t	e	f	l	g	c
c	l	g	e	f	t

~~ Use the cursor to read the practice sentences.

~~~ Instruct your student to write the letter that makes the sound that you dictate.

b   m   p   n   h   a

~~~~Next, you will read a few sentences to your student. The student will underline the sentences as you read, looping the key word as the student moves from left to right.

Before Page 77

Before beginning page 77, go through all of the vowels and review their short sound and their names (long sound). I recommend using letter magnets or tiles for this. You can make it into a game. Hide a letter magnet under your hand and say, "To free this letter from the trap, you have to say its name. If you listen closely, you'll hear the letter calling out its short sound as a clue." Pretend along with the child, and extend this game for as long as the child's interest holds. It's a good idea to simply let this game be the lesson for the day. Get out the animal figurines and pretend the tiger will eat Mr. A or Mrs. E if we cannot save them first.

(This game can and should be played over and over again until your child becomes bored with it. It's a fantastic review of the vowel sounds and prepares the child to take the next step in learning to read, seeing and hearing the fluidity of the letters as they change sounds throughout our vast collection of English words.)

*Notice: We are introducing the silent 'e.' Tell your student that sometimes a silent 'e' at the end of a word makes a vowel say its name. (Sometimes a silent 'e' has a different job in the word, but we are going to learn about that later.) Just like in our game above, the vowel gives a clue to the sound and the silent 'e' comes along to help us say its name (and free the poor vowel from the jaws of the crocodile...).

~Dictate the words below. Ask your student to say each sound as they trace the word that they hear. If there is a silent 'e,' underline it and draw an arrow below the word from the silent 'e' to the vowel that says its name.

at	ate	can	cane	mat	mate
man	mane	fad	fade	rat	rate

~~Use the cursor to read the practice words.

~ Dictate a sound for your student to trace.

g	b	e	c	t	l
e	g	l	b	c	t
t	b	g	l	e	c

~~ Use the cursor to read the practice sentences.

~~~ Instruct your student to write the letter they hear as you dictate these letter sounds.

qu	b	d	g	j	r

~~~~Next, you will read a few sentences to your student. The student will underline the sentences as you read, looping the key word as the student moves from left to right.

~Dictate the words below. Ask your student to say each sound as they trace the word that they hear. If there is a silent 'e,' underline it and draw an arrow below the word from the silent'e' to the vowel that says its name.

hid	hide	cap	cape	dim	dime
tap	tape	fin	fine	bit	bite

~~Use the cursor to read the practice words.

Page 80

~ Dictate a sound for your student to trace.

g	b	i	c	t	l
i	g	l	b	c	t
t	b	g	l	i	c

~~ Use the cursor to read the practice sentences.

~~~ Instruct your student to write the letter they hear as you dictate these letter sounds.

qu	z	k	g	y	r

~~~~Next, you will read a few sentences to your student. The student will underline the sentences as you read, looping the key word as the student moves from left to right.

Page 81

~Dictate the words below. Ask your student to say each sound as they trace the word that they hear. If there is a silent 'e,' underline it and draw an arrow below the word from the silent 'e' to the vowel that says its name.

Pin	pine	not	note	rob	robe
Rip	ripe	hop	hope	Sam	same

~~Use the cursor to read the practice words.

~ Dictate a sound for your student to trace.

k	b	c	l	g	i
i	g	k	c	b	l
l	c	k	i	g	b

~~ Use the cursor to read the practice sentences.

~~~ Instruct your student to write the letter they hear as you dictate these letter sounds.

x	h	w	t	p	n

~~~~Next, you will read a few sentences to your student. The student will underline the sentences as you read, looping the key word as the student moves from left to right.

Page 83

~Dictate the words below. Ask your student to say each sound as they trace the word that they hear. If there is a silent 'e,' underline it and draw an arrow below the word from the silent'e' to the vowel that says its name.

Us	use	tub	tube	cub	cube
Mop	mope	win	wine	rid	ride

~~Use the cursor to read the practice words.

~ Dictate a sound for your student to trace.

k	b	g	h	c	i
h	i	k	b	c	g
b	k	h	i	g	c

~~ Use the cursor to read the practice words. Notice the third line is a sentence. We begin a sentence with a capital letter and end it with a period.

~~~ Instruct your student to write the letter they hear as you dictate these letter sounds.

h	v	s	w	d	f

~~~~Next, you will read a few sentences to your student. The student will underline the sentences as you read, looping the key word as the student moves from left to right.

Page 85

~Decode the words below together. Note the silent 'e' first and move sound-by-sound, allowing the child to hear the word. Then instruct the student to trace the word, saying each *sound* as they trace. (*Whisper "silent e" as you trace the silent 'e.'*)

wade   safe   bake   side   wide

tide   poke   joke   tune

~~Use the cursor to read the practice words.

Page 86

~ Dictate a sound for your student to trace.

b	d	h	k	i	c
d	i	b	h	k	c
c	d	i	h	b	k

~~ Use the cursor to read the practice sentences.

~~~ Instruct your student to write the letter they hear as you dictate these letter sounds.

y	m	r	s	n	j

~~~~Next, you will read a few sentences to your student. The student will underline the sentences as you read, looping the key word as the student moves from left to right.

~Decode the words below together. Note the silent 'e' first and move sound-by-sound, allowing the child to hear the word. Then instruct the student to trace the word, saying each *sound* as they trace. (*Whisper "silent e" as you trace the silent 'e.'*)

rake   life   came   June   mole

gate   wipe   cave   tale

~~Use the cursor to read the practice words.

~ Dictate a sound for your student to trace.

d	i	b	h	k	p
P	d	i	h	b	k
b	d	h	k	i	p

~~ Use the cursor to read the practice sentences.

~~~ Instruct your student to write the letter they hear as you dictate these letter sounds.

y	qu	r	s	t	j

~~~~Next, you will read a few sentences to your student. The student will underline the sentences as you read, looping the key word as the student moves from left to right.

~Decode the words below together. Note the silent 'e' first and move sound-by-sound, allowing the child to hear the word. Then instruct the student to trace the word, saying each *sound* as they trace. (*Whisper "silent e" as you trace the silent 'e.'*)

wake   vine   nine   cure   pure

live   late   time   make

~~Use the cursor to read the practice words.

~ Dictate a sound for your student to trace.

d	o	i	p	h	k
h	i	k	o	p	d
k	p	d	o	h	i

~~ Use the cursor to read the practice sentences.

~~~ Instruct your student to write the letter they hear as you dictate these letter sounds.

a	e	o	u	f	r

~~~~Next, you will read a few sentences to your student. The student will underline the sentences as you read, looping the key word as the student moves from left to right.

~Decode the words below together. Note the silent 'e' first and move sound-by-sound, allowing the child to hear the word. Then instruct the student to trace the word, saying each *sound* as they trace. (*Whisper "silent e" as you trace the silent 'e.'*)

     sale   pole   mine   core   tore

         sore   fire   wire   tire

~~Use the cursor to read the practice words.

~ Dictate a sound for your student to trace.

d	k	p	o	j	h
j	p	k	o	d	h
k	d	o	p	h	j

~~ Use the cursor to read the practice sentences.

~~~ Instruct your student to write the letter they hear as you dictate these letter sounds.

g	e	u	l	m	v

~~~~Next, you will read a few sentences to your student. The student will underline the sentences as you read, looping the key word as the student moves from left to right.

~Decode the words below together. Note the silent 'e' first and move sound-by-sound, allowing the child to hear the word. Then instruct the student to trace the word, saying each *sound* as they trace. (*Whisper "silent e" as you trace the silent 'e.'*)

wore   more   home   five   base

game   lake   rope   pile

~~Use the cursor to read the practice words.

~ Dictate a sound for your student to trace.

w	d	j	p	o	h
h	d	j	w	p	o
j	o	w	d	p	h

~~ Use the cursor to read the practice sentences.

~~~ Instruct your student to write the letter they hear as you dictate these letter sounds.

K	i	f	e	n	u

~~~~Next, you will read a few sentences to your student. The student will underline the sentences as you read, looping the key word as the student moves from left to right.

~Decode the words below together. Note the silent 'e' first and move sound-by-sound, allowing the child to hear the word. Then instruct the student to trace the word, saying each *sound* as they trace. (*Whisper "silent e" as you trace the silent 'e.'*)

name   wife   mule   cure   hire

save   mile   take   gave

~~Use the cursor to read the practice words.

~ Dictate a sound for your student to trace.

o	j	o	w	d	p
w	u	o	p	j	d
p	o	u	j	d	p

~~ Use the cursor to read the practice sentences.

~~~ Instruct your student to write the letter they hear as you dictate these letter sounds.

i	y	e	s	z	x

~~~~Next, you will read a few sentences to your student. The student will underline the sentences as you read, looping the key word as the student moves from left to right.

Placement Test

Dictate the letters given below by their sounds. Instruct your student to write the letter that makes the sound that they hear. If your student cannot identify and write each letter as they hear its sound, review the letters until they can. Do not move on until they are confident!

qu p a l z m w o s k x

n c b d j e l r u f h v g t y

Use a cursor to read the words on page 98 in the student manual. If your student needs help on more than 3 words in this section, go back and repeat pages 69 through the end.

Congratulations! Your student is now a reader!

The next steps in reading include learning the phonograms and complex spelling patterns. After completing this Reading and Writing Program, you have a good understanding of how your student learns. Be confident in giving your student personalized lessons in small, consistent increments. Happy Reading!!!

a	b
c	d
e	f
g	h
i	j
k	l
m	n

o	p
q	r
s	t
u	v
w	x
y	z

A	B
C	D
E	F
G	H
I	J
K	L
M	N

O	P
Q	R
S	T
U	V
W	X
Y	Z

a	b
c	d
e	f
g	h
i	j
k	l
m	n
o	p

q	r
s	t
u	v
w	x
y	z

A	B
C	D
E	F
G	H
I	J
K	L
M	N
O	P

Q	R
S	T
U	V
W	X
Y	Z

Lightning Source UK Ltd.
Milton Keynes UK
UKHW050753130722
405793UK00007B/418

9 781300 385172